Dear Parents:

Congratulations! Your child is taking the first steps on an exciting journey. The destination? Independent reading!

STEP INTO READING® will help your child get there. The program offers five steps to reading success. Each step includes fun stories and colorful art or photographs. In addition to original fiction and books with favorite characters, there are Step into Reading Non-Fiction Readers, Phonics Readers and Boxed Sets, Sticker Readers, and Comic Readers—a complete literacy program with something to interest every child.

Learning to Read, Step by Step!

Ready to Read   Preschool–Kindergarten
• big type and easy words • rhyme and rhythm • picture clues
For children who know the alphabet and are eager to begin reading.

Reading with Help   Preschool–Grade 1
• basic vocabulary • short sentences • simple stories
For children who recognize familiar words and sound out new words with help.

Reading on Your Own   Grades 1–3
• engaging characters • easy-to-follow plots • popular topics
For children who are ready to read on their own.

Reading Paragraphs   Grades 2–3
• challenging vocabulary • short paragraphs • exciting stories
For newly independent readers who read simple sentences with confidence.

Ready for Chapters   Grades 2–4
• chapters • longer paragraphs • full-color art
For children who want to take the plunge into chapter books but still like colorful pictures.

STEP INTO READING® is designed to give every child a successful reading experience. The grade levels are only guides; children will progress through the steps at their own speed, developing confidence in their reading. The F&P Text Level on the back cover serves as another tool to help you choose the right book for your child.

Remember, a lifetime love of reading starts with a single step!

For Adelaide
and all the Swifties
—S.C.

For Clarissa and Caylee,
dream big and love fearlessly
—C.Q.

Text copyright © 2025 by Shana Corey
Cover art and interior illustrations copyright © 2025 by Chloe Quinn

All rights reserved. Published in the United States by Random House Children's Books,
a division of Penguin Random House LLC, 1745 Broadway, New York, NY 10019.

Step into Reading, Random House, and the Random House colophon are registered trademarks
of Penguin Random House LLC.

Visit us on the Web!
StepIntoReading.com
rhcbooks.com

Educators and librarians, for a variety of teaching tools, visit us at RHTeachersLibrarians.com

Library of Congress Cataloging-in-Publication Data is available upon request.
ISBN 979-8-217-03153-5 (hardcover) — ISBN 979-8-217-02955-6 (paperback) —
ISBN 979-8-217-02956-3 (lib. bdg.) — ISBN 979-8-217-02957-0 (ebook)

Printed in the United States of America
10 9 8 7 6 5 4 3 2 1
First Edition

This book has been officially leveled by using the F&P Text Level Gradient™ Leveling System.

TAYLOR SWIFT
SUPERSTAR!

by Shana Corey
illustrated by Chloe Quinn

Random House 🏠 New York

Taylor Swift was born on December 13, 1989, in Pennsylvania.

Taylor grew up
with her parents
and her younger brother.
They lived on a
Christmas tree farm!

Taylor helped
around the farm.
She rode horses.

She acted in plays,
and she wrote poems.

Taylor loved writing.
She won an award
for her poetry!

Taylor also loved music.
Country songs were
her favorite.

She liked how
they told stories.
Taylor wanted
to do that, too!

Taylor had big dreams.
She took
singing lessons.
She practiced a lot!

Taylor sang at fairs
and contests
and sports events.

Taylor learned
to play guitar.

She began to write
her own songs.
Her songs told
stories about her life.

Middle school
was hard for Taylor.
Kids were not always
nice to her.

She found comfort
in her music.

Taylor wanted
to follow her dreams.
Her family
wanted to help.

They moved
to Nashville, Tennessee.
There were lots of
music studios there.

Taylor got a music deal!

Taylor released
her first album!

The album featured
country music.
It included songs
she had written!

Taylor's next album was
called *Fearless*.
It won
Album of the Year!

Taylor became famous!
Her fans call
themselves Swifties.
They love Taylor,
and she loves them!

Taylor's fans want
to know all about her.
She hides codes
in her albums
for them to find.
The codes give
hints about her life!

Taylor kept
trying new things.
She released
her first pop album.
It was named *1989*—
the year she was born.

T.S.   1989

It was

her biggest hit yet!

23

Sometimes Taylor
faced setbacks.
But she worked hard
and did not give up.

Taylor became
a role model.
She believed in equality
for all people.
She used her platform
to speak for others.

Taylor started
her biggest tour yet
in 2023.
It was called
the Eras tour.

She sold out
giant stadiums
all over the world!

Fans of all ages
came together
during the tour.
Some went to shows.
Others watched
at movie theaters.

They traded
friendship bracelets.
They sang and danced.
Many even dressed
like Taylor!

Taylor Swift is
a legend
and a record breaker.

She makes history
and headlines.
She inspires millions
of people!

Taylor followed
her dreams.
Now it is your turn
to follow yours!